I FOUND IT

Jeremiah 29:13 (KJV)
And ye shall seek me, and find me, when ye shall search for me with all your heart.

And in searching, I found that HE was never lost, I was…

ROSEANNE WILSON

xulon PRESS

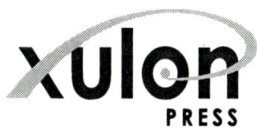

Copyright © 2011 by Roseanne Wilson

I Found It!
Jeremiah 29:13 (KJV) And ye shall seek me, and find me, when ye shall search for me with all your heart.
by Roseanne Wilson

Printed in the United States of America

ISBN 9781613797433

All rights reserved solely by the author. The author guarantees all contents are original and do not infringe upon the legal rights of any other person or work. No part of this book may be reproduced in any form without the permission of the author. The views expressed in this book are not necessarily those of the publisher.

Unless otherwise indicated, Bible quotations are taken from The HOLY BIBLE, NEW INTERNATIONAL VERSION®. Copyright © 1973, 1978, 1984, 2010 by Biblica. Used by permission of Zondervan; The Amplified® Bible (AMP), http://www.biblegateway.com. Copyright © 1954, 1958, 1962, 1964, 1965, 1987 by The Lockman Foundation. Used by permission. (www.Lockman.org); and The King James Version (KJV).

www.xulonpress.com

DEDICATION

In loving memory of all of my deceased siblings: Beulah, Earl, James, Caesar, Charles, Ruth, Clois, Laura, William, Joe Murray, Phay, and Brenda. I miss you!

To my husband, Jimmy Wilson who has been a constant in my life, and who has motivated me to finish this project. I love you!

To my only living brother, Shelton, even with his handicap, is such an inspiration with his undying perseverance. I'm glad you are here with me!

TABLE OF CONTENTS

ACKOWLEDGMENTS ix
HOW TO GET THE MOST FROM THIS BOOK xi
INTRODUCTION xiii
IN THE BEGINNING 17
LOVE 20
THE HOLY SPIRIT 22
WISDOM 27
THE TRANSFORMATION 29
TRUST 36
TRUTH 38
ASK, SEEK, KNOCK 40
LUCK VS. FAITH 44
TOLERANCE 47
THE JOURNEY 51
MARRIAGE 52
WHAT'S LOVE GOT TO DO WITH IT 55
DIVORCE 61
INTROSPECTION 65
THE GLORIOUS STATE: SINGLENESS 68
I SURRENDER ALL 71
THE END 75
A NEW BEGINNING—A NEW LIFE IN CHRIST 76
MY PRAYER FOR YOU 79

ACKNOWLEDGEMENTS

First, and foremost, with gratitude and thanks, I give all praise and honor to my Lord and Savior, Jesus the Christ. Through His infinite wisdom and unselfishness He has made available to me wisdom and knowledge, and understanding. In doing this, He has given to me the keys to the mysteries of the Kingdom of God through the inspiration of His *Holy Spirit* that rests, rules, and abides in me.

I give a multitude of thanks (which does not express the amount of gratitude I hold) to my Episcopal Pastor Dr. John A. Cherry, founding Pastor of From The Heart Church Ministries, Camp Springs, Maryland, and his elegant and lovely wife, Minister, Dr. Diana P. Cherry for their eloquent (albeit sometimes harsh), uncompromising and selfless admonishment in rendering "thus saith the Lord." Their outpouring love brought me to an understanding of God's love for me, and the sacrifice that was made for me by Christ Jesus.

Because of their clear and unadulterated communication of the understanding of the intent of the Scriptures (by way of the Greek and Hebrew), they taught me not only w*hat*, but w*hy* and h*ow*, to be who I was in Christ, and set me on a course to finding my purpose here on earth. It was their teachings of the Gospel that gave the Spirit of the Living God something to work with, both in and through me.

    It is with much love that I dedicate this book to my Mama and my Daddy, both who are long passed on, but who were pivotal in my becoming the person God had to work with. Although they were not much on talking, they were doers of the Word, living a life of much love. I was the one child who observed what was going on around me. Their example showed me what love was and how it could stand the test of time.

HOW TO GET THE MOST FROM THIS BOOK

As you read this book, you will find references to the Bible. Some are quoted fully while others are not. You will learn much more about the Christian mind if you keep a Bible handy to look up the references and read them, especially the suggested Scripture readings found throughout each chapter. It will help even further if you would read the verses before and after the referenced verses. And for an overall understanding of the context of the verses referenced, read the entire chapter.

INTRODUCTION

In my journey through life, I had to ask a lot of questions, and after my born again experience, all those questions were answered. You see, when I found God, through Jesus, the Christ, I found me!

As time went on I began learning more about who God was through Christ Jesus, and my "ah-ha" moments were constant. The light of knowledge began to shine, and my understanding was opened in such a way that even blew me away. I found that the working of the *Holy Spirit* was real, and free for the asking.

Even when we were cut off from the life of God, He loved us, and through the sacrificial death of Jesus on the cross, He has drawn us to Himself. It is He who first loved us when we did not know nor love Him—for the Spirit of God is *Love*. It is that love for us that caused him to sacrifice his Son on our behalf.

God gave his only begotten Son that we might have life, and have it more abundantly. That abundant life is for the present, not just for the hereafter. Romans 10:10 tells us that "if we confess with our mouth the Lord Jesus, and believe in our heart that God hath raised him from the dead, thou shalt be saved"; that belief is in the heart and confession is made with your mouth; and by it you will be saved.

Although I began my journey some 25 years ago, today, I am still growing because we never stop learning; the *Holy Spirit* is still illuminating.

You know, there is so much information out here in the world, a lot of facts; but after assimilating what was out there, I learned to use the Word of God as a barometer to bring truth into all situations.

It was after listening to both Oprah and Dr. Phil on their talk shows that caused me to contemplate some of the issues they discussed. I realized that they have become a billionaire and a millionaire, respectively, espousing words of wisdom and knowledge that did not begin with them (nor will they end with them). So, I decided to put down on paper that which is available to *ALL* of us *IF WE WANT IT*, and to tell you where to go to find it, so that *YOU TOO* can tap into everlasting and ever-evolving knowledge for your life's journey.

It is not my intention in this little book to take away the truths that have been espoused by Oprah and Dr. Phil, but to add to them, and to shed some light on others. Nor do I intend to give you all of "what thus saith the Lord" in this little book because it is impossible to do so in this vehicle, but I would suggest that you investigate it for yourself. For Scripture tells us that if we will seek God diligently, we will find him.

In this little book I want to get down to the crux of the matters at hand. Get down to that which is the foundation of *ALL LIFE,* and that which can be known to *ALL MEN.*

I asked the question, "what is missing from what both Oprah and Dr. Phil was telling me and others. There is a book out on the market entitled, "The Gospel According To Oprah," written by Marcia Z. Nelson[1]; but my intention for writing this book, is to give you the "Gospel according to the Gospel."

In the natural realm, when we are unsure of how things are put together or constructed, we reach for the instruction manual; and so it is in the spiritual realm. When we want to know how to live, who we are, and whose we are, we are to reach for the instruction manual for life from Him who created us in His image, and His likeness—the HOLY SCRIPTURES.

As Scripture tells us, there is no secret in Christ, nor is there anything new under the sun. It is available to everyone who seeks it. There is no need for a special password or handshake; you just need a willingness to accept Jesus as Lord and Savior of your life. You must be willing to accept the work that He has done for you through His death, burial, and resurrection, and allow God's *Holy Spirit* to take control of your thoughts and actions.

Scripture calls this the born again experience. In the Book of John, Jesus told Nicodemus that "You must be born again" (John 3:7, *NIV © 2010*), "born of water and the Spirit" (John 3:5, *NIV © 2010*). Of course, Nicodemus was a bit perplexed by Jesus' response (as some may be). This is not surprising, as Scripture tells us that the carnal or natural mind of man cannot discern the things of the Spirit.

*****

This little book is written for everyone, the believer and the non-believer alike. It is a book written to spark growth in knowing the one and only living God—a God who loved mankind so much that He sacrificed His only son after allowing Him to walk among us so that we could behold God's glory; manifested in human flesh as Jesus, the Christ.

This little book is written to serve as a catalyst to cause you to question who you are, where you are, and where you are going. It is a book for the young, old, male, female, rich or poor—a book for all mankind.

I'd like to preface this book by stating that my point of reference is the Holy Scriptures—for from its pages come knowledge, understanding and wisdom. It is my desire to impart this so-called *SECRET* to all of you.

The *SECRET* has been dissected and exposed. Within this book we will get down to the crux of the matter, that which is the foundation of *ALL LIFE,* and can be known to *ALL MEN.*

WELL, LET'S GET STARTED … IN THE BEGINNING …

IN THE BEGINNING

Genesis 1:1 (KJV)
In the beginning God created the heaven and the earth.

Genesis 1:21 (KJV)
And God created great whales, and every living creature that moveth, which the waters brought forth abundantly, after their kind, and every winged fowl after his kind: and God saw that it was good.

John 1 (KJV)
In the beginning was the Word, and the Word was with God, and the Word was God.

The same was in the beginning with God.

All things were made by him; and without him was not any thing made that was made.

In the beginning, humans were created in the image of God, the **SOURCE OF LIFE**, and in His likeness. The breath of life was blown into our nostrils. At that moment, God himself gifted us with our spirit. It is by our spirit that we are able to connect to Him; through His Son Jesus, the Christ, and whereby we are given access to His abundant riches, by the indwelling of His *Holy Spirit*. We are ultimately spirit, and we are housed in a body, with a mind that encompasses our will, intellect and emotions.

Scientist and those who practice the study of the brain and its function have surmised that "your brain is the most sophisticated, complex and miraculous piece of equipment ever known to humankind."

Have you ever wondered where does knowledge come from? Although scientists and those who study the human mind know the "mechanics" because of knowledge that has been given to them by God, they cannot explain the "how" or the "why." The only answer is "BUT GOD"; for He is sovereign, infinite, all-knowing, and omniscient. For we know that all things were created by Him, and that there is nothing new under the sun.

Genesis 1:26 (KJV)
And God said, Let us make man in our image, after our likeness: and let them have dominion over the fish of the sea, and over the fowl of the air, and over the cattle, and over all the earth, and over every creeping thing that creepeth upon the earth.

Genesis 2:1 (KJV)
Thus the heavens and the earth were finished, and all the host of them.

Genesis 2:7 (AMP)
Then the Lord God formed man from the dust of the ground and breathed into his nostrils the breath or spirit of life, and man became a living being.

*****

Ephesians 3:18-21 (KJV)
[We] May be able to comprehend with all saints what is the breadth, and length, and depth, and height;

And to know the love of Christ, which passeth knowledge, that ye might be filled with all the fulness of God.

Now unto him that is able to do exceeding abundantly above all that we ask or think, according to the power that worketh in us,

Unto him be glory in the church by Christ Jesus throughout all ages, world without end. Amen

LOVE

The first Commandment is that you love God with all your heart and mind, and the second is likened unto it—that you love your neighbor as yourself.

John 13:34-35 (KJV)
A new commandment I give unto you, That ye love one another; as I have loved you, that ye also love one another.

By this shall all men know that ye are my disciples, if ye have love one to another.

We were created to love one another and to care for one another. Society would have you believe that "self-preservation is the first law of nature." Who was it that came up with that saying anyway? (Oh, it was Samuel Butler.[2] Mr. Butler is an example of one who dissected his own truths and drew his own conclusions based on his life experiences, without consulting his creator.

1 John 4:6-8 (KJV)
We are of God: he that knoweth God heareth us; he that is not of God heareth not us. Hereby know we the spirit of truth, and the spirit of error.

Beloved, let us love one another: for love is of God; and every one that loveth is born of God, and knoweth God.

He that loveth not knoweth not God; for God is love.

The truth is, no man is an island, no man stands alone. We are our brother's keeper and when we show love and caring for our brother, it shows our love for God. For who can love God whom he has not seen, and not love his brother who he has seen?

Oh what poignant wording; what strong and unselfish thought; what powerful truth God has set forth into the universe for us humans. We humans, who were created a little lower than the angels—beings whose only job is to worship God, the Father, and to minister unto us.

It is amazing to me how the Father loves us in spite of us. It has nothing to do with what we do outside of him, but who we are in Him. Once we are in Him, His Spirit will guide us to do right. Hallelujah!

Oh so sweet to trust in Jesus and to take him at his word. There is a song that says it so beautifully, "Oh, how I love Jesus because he first loved me."

1 John 4:19-21 (KJV)
We love him, because he first loved us.

If a man say, I love God, and hateth his brother, he is a liar: for he that loveth not his brother whom he hath seen, how can he love God whom he hath not seen?

And this commandment have we from him, That he who loveth God love his brother also.

THE HOLY SPIRIT

John 14:25-26 (NIV © 2010)
All this I have spoken while still with you.

But the Counselor, the Holy Spirit, whom the Father will send in my name, will teach you all things and will remind you of everything I have said to you.

Yes, the *Holy Spirit*, or as some might say, *the Holy Ghost*, (or as it's known in the study of metaphysics as the *"Christ Consciousness"* or *"God Consciousness"*), is to lead and guide us into all truths. Through whichever way you may see it, speak it, or have heard it, He (the *Holy Spirit*) was sent from the Father and the Son, so that we would not have to go through life blindly, experiencing *ALL* the hardships and failures unto death, while living in this earthly realm.

Matthew 5:10 (AMP)
Blessed and happy and enviably fortunate and spiritually prosperous (in the state in which the born-again child of God enjoys and finds satisfaction in God's favor and salvation, regardless of his outward conditions) are those who are persecuted for righteousness' sake (for being and doing right), for theirs is the kingdom of heaven!

John 3:34 (AMP)
For since He Whom God has sent speaks the words of God [proclaims God's own message], God does not give Him His Spirit sparingly or by measure, but boundless is the gift God makes of His Spirit!

A lot of talk has been given to the earthly realm, but there is a higher realm for the spirit, and that is the heavenly realm. It is the realm where all knowledge exists, where all truth exists, where Jesus exists. It is in this realm that our spirits communicate with the Spirit of the Living God.

In Matthew 3:1-3, John the Baptist came on the scene saying, "*Repent ye: for the kingdom of heaven is at hand.*" Meaning we were about to experience the coming of the Word of God, in the person of Jesus, the Christ, in the flesh, and that all we have to do is ask for forgiveness of our sins, and be born again. That is, to allow the Spirit of God to commune with our spirit.

Mark 1:15 (AMP)
And saying, The [appointed period of] time is fulfilled (completed), and the kingdom of God is at hand; repent (have a change of mind which issues in regret for past sins and in change of conduct for the better) and believe (trust in, rely on, and adhere to) the good news (the Gospel).

Acts 2:38 (AMP)
And Peter answered them, Repent (change your views and purpose to accept the will of God in your inner selves instead of rejecting it) and be baptized, every one of you, in the name of Jesus Christ for the forgiveness of and release from your sins; and you shall receive the gift of the Holy Spirit.

Acts 2:39 (AMP)
For the promise [of the Holy Spirit] is to and for you and your children, and to and for all that are far away, [even] to and for as many as the Lord our God invites and bids to come to Himself.

Acts 4:31 (AMP)
And when they had prayed, the place in which they were assembled was shaken; and they were all filled with the Holy Spirit, and they continued to speak the Word of God with freedom and boldness and courage.

Acts 5:32 (AMP)
And we are witnesses of these things, and the Holy Spirit is also, Whom God has bestowed on those who obey Him.

Acts 7:55 (AMP)
But he, full of the Holy Spirit and controlled by Him, gazed into heaven and saw the glory (the splendor and majesty) of God, and Jesus standing at God's right hand.

Acts 10:38 (AMP)
How God anointed and consecrated Jesus of Nazareth with the [Holy] Spirit and with strength and ability and power; how He went about doing good and, in particular, curing all who were harassed and oppressed by [the power of] the devil, for God was with Him.

Acts 15:8 (AMP)
And God, Who is acquainted with and understands the heart, bore witness to them, giving them the Holy Spirit as He also did to us.

I can only speak on that which I know and understand; and I do know this one thing: the Spirit of the one and only living God, Jesus, is real, and that His Spirit, which is known as the *Holy Spirit*, will dwell in each and every one of us, if we allow Him to. Romans 10 gives us an invitation to that place of enlightenment:

Romans 10: 9-11 (NIV © 2010)
That if you confess with your mouth, "Jesus is Lord," and believe in your heart that God raised him from the dead, you will be saved. For it is with your heart that you believe and are justified, and it is with your mouth that you confess and are saved. As the Scripture says, "Anyone who trusts in him will never be put to shame."

Paul, an Apostle of Jesus Christ, exhorts us to be *"transformed by the renewing of our mind*—our thoughts, our words, our deeds. That mindset is the *Christ Consciousness*. The transforming power is as near as our mouths when we accept God's gift of His Son, and the sacrifice he made for us in his death, burial and resurrection. The blessed gift of the *Holy Spirit* will come to live in us after the born again experience, and that which beckons for our command to rise up.

Romans 12:2 (NIV © 2010)
Therefore, I urge you, brothers and sisters, in view of God's mercy, to offer your bodies as a living sacrifice, holy and pleasing to God—this is your true and proper worship.

Do not conform to the pattern of this world, but be transformed by the renewing of your mind. Then you will be able to test and approve what God's will is— his good, pleasing and perfect will.

Apostle Paul declares:

Philippians 1:6 (KJV)
Being confident of this very thing, that he which hath begun a good work in you will perform it until the day of Jesus Christ.

WISDOM

Proverbs 4:5 (KJV)
Get wisdom, get understanding: forget it not; neither decline from the words of my mouth.

Proverbs 4:7 (KJV)
Wisdom is the principal thing; therefore get wisdom: and with all thy getting get understanding.

Psalm 119:104 (KJV)
Through thy precepts I get understanding: therefore I hate every false way.

What we must do is dig deep into the sea of knowledge that lies within us. We must ask the right questions in order to get the right answers. We must learn how to listen to that soft voice when it speaks to us—for He will speak. We must follow through on guidance and direction when it is given to us.

Those who pontificate with such self-assurance, through great eloquence and brilliance, have not been given any more than you have. Some have acquired knowledge through education and some through experiences in life. These have grasped the elementary things of life and have built upon them.

Without wisdom, which is taking what we know and understand and using it for our benefit, we cannot grow and mature in the things of life—things which have been given to us by the God of all knowledge, through Jesus, the Christ. Others have tapped into the **SOURCE OF LIFE** without acknowledging the true source of their knowledge, wisdom, and understanding.

Proverbs 3:13 (KJV)
Happy is the man that findeth wisdom, and the man that getteth understanding.

Proverbs 15:32 (KJV)
He that refuseth instruction despiseth his own soul: but he that heareth reproof getteth understanding.

Proverbs 16:16 (KJV)
How much better is it to get wisdom than gold! and to get understanding rather to be chosen than silver!

Proverbs 19:8 (KJV)
He that getteth wisdom loveth his own soul: he that keepeth understanding shall find good.

ʚ ɞ
THE TRANSFORMATION

The transformation from our old self to our new self (which began when we established a relationship with God through Jesus Christ), must begin with our acknowledgment that we are weak, fearful, and uncommitted within ourselves. We must begin the journey of:

KNOWING SELF…

To truly know yourself, you must know that you are spirit, that you reside in a physical body, and that you have a soul, consisting of your mind, will, and emotions.

To begin to acquire the knowledge that is available to you (and all of us) you must "know thyself" and trust in the **SOURCE OF LIFE** (God).

Psalm 139:1-14 (KJV)
O lord, thou hast searched me, and known me.

Thou knowest my downsitting and mine uprising, thou understandest my thought afar off.

Thou compassest my path and my lying down, and art acquainted with all my ways.

*For there is not a word in my tongue, but, lo, O LORD,
thou knowest it altogether.*

Thou hast beset me behind and before, and laid thine hand upon me.

*Such knowledge is too wonderful for me; it is high,
I cannot attain unto it.*

*Whither shall I go from thy spirit? or whither shall I flee
from thy presence?*

*If I ascend up into heaven, thou art there: if I make my bed in
hell, behold, thou art there.*

*If I take the wings of the morning, and dwell in the uttermost
parts of the sea;*

Even there shall thy hand lead me, and thy right hand shall hold me.

*If I say, Surely the darkness shall cover me; even the
night shall be light about me.*

*Yea, the darkness hideth not from thee; but the night shineth as the
day: the darkness and the light are both alike to thee.*

*For thou hast possessed my reins: thou hast covered me
in my mother's womb.*

*I will praise thee; for I am fearfully and wonderfully made: marvellous
are thy works; and that my soul knoweth right well.*

Genesis 1:26 (KJV)
And God said, Let us make man in our image, after our likeness: and let them have dominion over the fish of the sea, and over the fowl of the air, and over the cattle, and over all the earth, and over every creeping thing that creepeth upon the earth.

Psalm 100:3 (KJV)
Know ye that the LORD he is God: it is he that hath made us, and not we ourselves; we are his people, and the sheep of his pasture.

DEVELOPING SELF

Development begins with knowing exactly who you are, that you are more than what you or others see with the natural eye. You are mind, body, and spirit. It is imperative that we align our minds and our spirits so that our bodies follow. First and foremost, we must align our spirits with the Spirit of God, so that we may be led by His Word and His truth.

Development of self requires introspection. We must take a hard look inside, deep into even the hidden places of our lives and be honest enough with ourselves to clean house. For God knows all and sees all. This cleansing must take place so we can overturn and overcome the "sin that so easily hinders us" (that sin we will to do, but which we know not to do.) We must become, inside and out, the person that God, our Creator, wants us to be. It allows us to live out that old cliché, what you see is what you get.

You see, we all have a purpose and a destiny that was designed even before our births, and it's up to us to find the path to that destiny, and to live in purpose.

Matthew 6:33 (KJV)
But seek ye first the kingdom of God, and his righteousness; and all these things shall be added unto you.

Romans 12:1-3 (KJV)
I beseech you therefore, brethren, by the mercies of God, that ye present your bodies a living sacrifice, holy, acceptable unto God, which is your reasonable service.

And be not conformed to this world: but be ye transformed by the renewing of your mind, that ye may prove what is that good, and acceptable, and perfect, will of God.

For I say, through the grace given unto me, to every man that is among you, not to think of himself more highly than he ought to think; but to think soberly, according as God hath dealt to every man the measure of faith.

Mark 4:11 (KJV)
And he said unto them, Unto you it is given to know the mystery of the kingdom of God: but unto them that are without, all these things are done in parables:

Romans 8:1-14 (KJV)
There is therefore now no condemnation to them which are in Christ Jesus, who walk not after the flesh, but after the Spirit.

For the law of the Spirit of life in Christ Jesus hath made me free from the law of sin and death.

what the law could not do, in that it was weak through the flesh, God sending his own Son in the likeness of sinful flesh, and for sin, condemned sin in the flesh:

the righteousness of the law might be fulfilled in us, who walk not after the flesh, but after the Spirit.

they that are after the flesh do mind the things of the flesh; but they that are after the Spirit the things of the Spirit.

to be carnally minded is death; but to be spiritually minded is life and peace.
the carnal mind is enmity against God: for it is not subject to the law of God, neither indeed can be.

then they that are in the flesh cannot please God.

But ye are not in the flesh, but in the Spirit, if so be that the Spirit of God dwell in you. Now if any man have not the Spirit of Christ, he is none of his.

And if Christ be in you, the body is dead because of sin; but the Spirit is life because of righteousness.

But if the Spirit of him that raised up Jesus from the dead dwell in you, he that raised up Christ from the dead shall also quicken your mortal bodies by his Spirit that dwelleth in you.

Therefore, brethren, we are debtors, not to the flesh, to live after the flesh.

For if ye live after the flesh, ye shall die: but if ye through the Spirit do mortify the deeds of the body, ye shall live.

For as many as are led by the Spirit of God, they are the sons of God.

Ephesians 1:8-10 KJV)
Wherein he hath abounded toward us in all wisdom and prudence;

Having made known unto us the mystery of his will, according to his good pleasure which he hath purposed in himself:

That in the dispensation of the fulness of times he might gather together in one all things in Christ, both which are in heaven, and which are on earth; even in him:

ACCEPTING SELF

The next step in this transformation is to accept what you have learned about yourself, and make a decision to let go of the old thoughts, words and deeds that accumulate to form your psychological makeup. Within this makeup lie your personality and habits. At this point, it is time to measure what you found in those hidden places within you against the Word of God—the compass for your life.

Jeremiah 31:3 (KJV)
The LORD hath appeared of old unto me, saying, Yea, I have loved thee with an everlasting love: therefore with lovingkindness have I drawn thee.

John 3:15-16 (KJV)
That whosoever believeth in him should not perish, but have eternal life.

For God so loved the world, that he gave his only begotten Son, that whosoever believeth in him should not perish, but have everlasting life.

John 5:30 (KJV)
I can of mine own self do nothing: as I hear, I judge: and my judgment is just; because I seek not mine own will, but the will of the Father which hath sent me.

Just as Jesus could do nothing without his Father, nor can we. We may go through life thinking that it is only us who are making things happen, or becoming known as a self-made man/woman, but in the end it is all vanity. Even the richest man ever known, King Solomon, came to that realization.

Ecclesiates 1:12-15 (AMP)
I, the Preacher, have been king over Israel in Jerusalem.

And I applied myself by heart and mind to seek and search out by [human] wisdom all human activity under heaven. It is a miserable business which God has given to the sons of man with which to busy themselves.

I have seen all the works that are done under the sun, and behold, all is vanity, a striving after the wind and a feeding on wind.

What is crooked cannot be made straight, and what is defective and lacking cannot be counted.

Ecclesiastes 12:13-14 (AMP)
All has been heard; the end of the matter is: Fear God [revere and worship Him, knowing that He is] and keep His commandments, for this is the whole of man [the full, original purpose of his creation, the object of God's providence, the root of character, the foundation of all happiness, the adjustment to all inharmonious circumstances and conditions under the sun] and the whole [duty] for every man.

For God shall bring every work into judgment, with every secret thing, whether it is good or evil.

TRUST

Proverbs 3:5-6 (NIV © 2010)
Trust in the Lord with all your heart and lean not on your own understanding; in all your ways acknowledge him, and he will make your paths straight.

S urprised? Don't be. In Deuteronomy 30:19-20 (*NIV © 2010*), God told the children of Israel:

This day I call heaven and earth as witnesses against you that I have set before you life and death, blessings and curses. Now choose life, so that you and your children may live and that you may love the Lord your God, listen to his voice, and hold fast to him. For the Lord is your life and He will give you many years in the land he swore to give to your fathers, Abraham, Isaac and Jacob.

The Old Testament consists of stories or examples of the relationship between God and His children. We read it and learn the character and integrity of a faithful God. There are countless examples of success, failure, joy, and lamentation from both those who learned the hard way, and those who were favored because of their unquestioned obedience to righteousness.

It is through trust and belief in God that we are brought to a place of unity, a place of agreement, which gives us access to wisdom and understanding.

Growth and maturity in spiritual things, through a relationship with the one and only true God, through Jesus, the Christ, and by His *Holy Spirit* will take you to higher heights and deeper depths.

Romans 8:39 (KJV)
Nor height, nor depth, nor any other creature, shall be able to separate us from the love of God, which is in Christ Jesus our Lord.

Romans 11:33 (KJV)
O the depth of the riches both of the wisdom and knowledge of God! How unsearchable are his judgments, and his ways past finding out!

TRUTH

What is *Truth*? One may say that it is an individual's opinion of what's best only for him or her. Due to our belief that what's good for one is not good for another, we tend to draw conclusions based upon selfishness.

The truth about *Truth* is that it is the same for everyone, and is for the good of everyone. *Truth* comes out of the character and attributes of God and His Word. *Truth* can be proven through the test of time. It is always best to receive truth sooner than later, because the sooner you receive it and apply it, the sooner you will mature. *Truth* always stands on a solid foundation and never changes—it is infallible.

KNOW THIS…

Psalm 119:142 (NKJV)
Your righteousness is an everlasting righteousness, and Your law is truth.

Psalm 139:13-15 (AMP)
For You did form my inward parts; You did knit me together in my mother's womb.

I will confess and praise You for You are fearful and wonderful and for the awful wonder of my birth! Wonderful are Your works, and that my inner self knows right well.

My frame was not hidden from You when I was being formed in secret [and] intricately and curiously wrought [as if embroidered with various colors] in the depths of the earth [a region of darkness and mystery].

John 1:17 (AMP)
For while the Law was given through Moses, grace (unearned, undeserved favor and spiritual blessing) and truth came through Jesus Christ.

You are beautifully and wonderfully made. You are made in the image and likeness of an Almighty God who knew what He was doing when He created you. By being made in His image, He has given you the ability to conform to His character. By being made in His likeness, He has given you the power to be like Him.

Learn to love yourself by getting to know the God who created you. Learn to forgive yourself by getting to know the God who created you. To know Him is to love Him; and when you find Him, you will find yourself.

When you form or build an intimate relationship with the God of truth, you will begin to see the light and your understanding will be opened up. I am not talking about a relationship with "the man upstairs" (as some say), or a relationship with an unknown God, but a relationship with the one who is as near as your mouth.

ASK, SEEK, KNOCK

Matthew 7:7-8 (AMP)
Keep on asking and it will be given you; keep on seeking and you will find; keep on knocking [reverently] and [the door] will be opened to you.

For everyone who keeps on asking receives; and he who keeps on seeking finds; and to him who keeps on knocking, [the door] will be opened.

Luke 11:9 (AMP)
So I say to you, Ask and keep on asking and it shall be given you; seek and keep on seeking and you shall find; knock and keep on knocking and the door shall be opened to you.

ASK...

James 1:5-8 (AMP)
If any of you is deficient in wisdom, let him ask of the giving God [Who gives] to everyone liberally and ungrudgingly, without reproaching or faultfinding, and it will be given him.

Only it must be in faith that he asks with no wavering (no hesitating, no doubting). For the one who wavers (hesitates, doubts) is like the billowing surge out at sea that is blown hither and thither and tossed by the wind.

For truly, let not such a person imagine that he will receive anything [he asks for] from the Lord,

[For being as he is] a man of two minds (hesitating, dubious, irresolute),
[he is] unstable and unreliable and uncertain about everything [he thinks, feels, decides].

We have long been told that we should not "question God." But He has instructed us to ask for what we want to know, have, and do. It is only in the asking that we receive the answers.

SEEK…

Matthew 6:33 (AMP)
But seek (aim at and strive after) first of all His kingdom and His righteousness (His way of doing and being right), and then all these things taken together will be given you besides.

James 1:2-4 (AMP)
Consider it wholly joyful, my brethren, whenever you are enveloped in or encounter trials of any sort or fall into various temptations.

Be assured and understand that the trial and proving of your faith bring out endurance and steadfastness and patience.

But let endurance and steadfastness and patience have full play and do a thorough work, so that you may be [people] perfectly and fully developed [with no defects], lacking in nothing.

The "things" Scripture speaks of include: understanding, wisdom, knowledge, righteousness, holiness, and most of all wholeness—not just material things. As John the Baptist proclaimed on his entrance on the scene:

Matthew 3:1-3 (KJV)
In those days came John the Baptist, preaching in the wilderness of Judaea,

And saying, Repent ye: for the kingdom of heaven is at hand.

For this is he that was spoken of by the prophet Esaias, saying, The voice of one crying in the wilderness, Prepare ye the way of the Lord, make his paths straight.

Jesus also proclaimed:

Mark 1:14-15 (KJV)
Now after that John was put in prison, Jesus came into Galilee, preaching the gospel of the kingdom of God,

And saying, The time is fulfilled, and the kingdom of God is at hand: repent ye, and believe the gospel.

John the Baptist and Jesus were letting us know that our access to an amazing transformation of mind, body, and spirit is at our disposal, just for the asking.

KNOCK...

Knock on the door of heaven—that place where the answers are. Knocking implies calling God at his Word; for whatever He has promised, He is faithful and stands ready to perform it.

Matthew 6:33 (KJV)
But seek ye first the kingdom of God, and his righteousness; and all these things shall be added unto you.

Ephesians 3:9 (KJV)
And to make all men see what is the fellowship of the mystery, which from the beginning of the world hath been hid in God, who created all things by Jesus Christ.

Behold (look), see, and hear—it's there for the asking.

LUCK vs. FAITH

2 Corinthians 5:7 (AMP)
For we walk by faith [we regulate our lives and conduct ourselves by our conviction or belief respecting man's relationship to God and divine things, with trust and holy fervor; thus we walk] not by sight or appearance.

Luck, by its very nature, is capricious and arbitrary because it is based on nothing more than changing circumstances.

Luck is opportunity and preparation; being in the right place at the right time; where the two shall meet.

Luck is always happen chance. It is the mindset of a gambler, or a dare devil. Both of them are wishing for something to happen or for things to go the way they want.

Faith is living in the hope of receiving that which you expect to receive. Hope is inherent in your faith. It is having expectations for that which you envision with your heart. Hope is that which we fully expect to receive.

Scripture says:

Proverbs 13:12 (AMP)
Hope deferred makes the heart sick, but when the desire is fulfilled,
it is a tree of life.

Hebrews 11:1,3 (AMP)
NOW FAITH is the assurance (the confirmation, the title deed)
of the things [we] hope for, being the proof of things [we] do not
see and the conviction of their reality [faith perceiving
as real fact what is not revealed to the senses].

By faith we understand that the worlds
[during the successive ages] were framed (fashioned, put in order,
and equipped for their intended purpose) by the word of God,
so that what we see was not made out of things which are visible.

Faith has nothing to do with the tangible, for with the tangible you do not need faith because you can see it, touch it, and feel it.

Faith overrides luck. Faith is ever-present while luck is based on changing circumstances.

Isaiah 30:18 (AMP)
And therefore the Lord [earnestly] waits [expecting, looking, and
longing] to be gracious to you; and therefore He lifts Himself up,
that He may have mercy on you and show loving-kindness to you.
For the Lord is a God of justice.
Blessed (happy, fortunate, to be envied) are all those who [earnestly]
wait for Him, who expect and look and long for Him [for His
victory, His favor, His love, His peace,
His joy, and His matchless, unbroken companionship]!

Psalm 27:13-14 (AMP)
[What, what would have become of me] had I not believed that I would see the Lord's goodness in the land of the living!

Wait and hope for and expect the Lord; be brave and of good courage and let your heart be stout and enduring. Yes, wait for and hope for and expect the Lord.

Moving in your faith in God and his righteousness is a sure bet; it's like money in the bank. By doing so, it gives you a blessed assurance. Consider trusting in God and His goodness now.

TOLERANCE

Society would have us believe that tolerance is about rising above the fray or taking the high road—a moral higher ground. In Scripture we are told to live amidst the "fray," to meet others where they are. It is this gesture that demonstrates our love for one another. Tolerance is *accepting the person*, but not the sinful acts that they perpetrate upon themselves and upon others. It is, in due time, your opportunity to express truth to those who are in your sphere of influence who are living outside of God's best for their life.

1 Corinthians 6:15-20 (KJV)
Know ye not that your bodies are the members of Christ?
shall I then take the members of Christ, and make them the
members of an harlot? God forbid.

What? know ye not that he which is joined to an harlot is one body?
for two, saith he, shall be one flesh.
But he that is joined unto the Lord is one spirit.

Flee fornication. Every sin that a man doeth is without the body;
but he that committeth fornication sinneth against his own body.

What? know ye not that your body is the temple of the Holy Ghost which is in you, which ye have of God, and ye are not your own?

For ye are bought with a price: therefore glorify God in your body, and in your spirit, which are God's.

It's ironic how Oprah and Dr. Phil will adamantly stand their ground against selfishness, abuse (verbal and physical), stealing, murdering, gossiping, smoking, gambling, and other sins of the flesh. But when it comes to the sins of the soul, those sins of the flesh that Scripture tells us will reap their own destruction, they condone. These sins include homosexuality, fornication, cohabitation, masturbation—the lust of the flesh, the lust of the eye, and the pride of life, to name a few.

1 John 2:16 (KJV)
For all that is in the world, the lust of the flesh, and the lust of the eyes, and the pride of life, is not of the Father, but is of the world.

1 Corinthians 6:9-12 (KJV)
Know ye not that the unrighteous shall not inherit the kingdom of God?

Be not deceived: neither fornicators, nor idolaters, nor adulterers, nor effeminate, nor abusers of themselves with mankind,

Nor thieves, nor covetous, nor drunkards, nor revilers, nor extortioners, shall inherit the kingdom of God.

And such were some of you: but ye are washed, but ye are sanctified, but ye are justified in the name of the Lord Jesus, and by the Spirit of our God.

All things are lawful unto me, but all things are not expedient: all things are lawful for me, but I will not be brought under the power of any.

Hebrews 13:4 (NIV © 2010)
Marriage should be honored by all, and the marriage bed kept pure, for God will judge the adulterer and the sexually immoral.

Galatians 6:8 (NIV © 2010)
For he that soweth to his flesh shall of the flesh reap corruption; but he that soweth to the Spirit shall of the Spirit reap life everlasting.

Scripture tells us that there is no weight when it comes to disobedience against Jehovah, God. In other words, sin is sin. There is no gray area.

1 John 5:17 (KJV)
All unrighteousness is sin: and there is a sin not unto death.

Deuteronomy 25:14-16 (KJV)
Thou shalt not have in thine house divers measures, a great and a small.

But thou shalt have a perfect and just weight, a perfect and just measure shalt thou have: that thy days may be lengthened in the land which the LORD thy God giveth thee.

For all that do such things, and all that do unrighteously, are an abomination unto the LORD thy God.

As humans, we must be born of the *Spirit* so that we may be in the position to judge unrighteousness. This judgment is done out of love, one for another.

John 7:24 (KJV)
Judge not according to the appearance, but judge righteous judgment.

Psalm 37:29-31 (KJV)
The righteous shall inherit the land, and dwell therein for ever.
The mouth of the righteous speaketh wisdom, and his tongue talketh of judgment.
The law of his God is in his heart; none of his steps shall slide.

THE JOURNEY

The foundation is now set and the groundwork covered. The remainder of this book will take you on a journey to the end of what some of us would call the most important decision in our lives, *MARRIAGE*, and then return you to the *SINGLE STATE* from which you began. This may seem backwards but just as God has predestined us to become His children and has come to show us the way (through his Word and His Spirit); so too, the following chapters will point you forward, and intentionally back to the beginning of your singleness.

ℰℴ ℭℛ
MARRIAGE

You've probably heard, "after the honeymoon, then comes the marriage." Let's look at marriage with a discerning eye to understand just what it entails. First and foremost, it begins with choosing the right person.

2 Corinthians 6:14 (KJV)
Do not be unequally yoked with unbelievers. For what partnership has righteousness with lawlessness? Or what fellowship has light with darkness?

Ecclesiastes 9:9 (NIV © 2010)
Enjoy life with the wife whom you love, all the days of your vain life that he has given you under the sun, because that is your portion in life and in your toil at which you toil under the sun.

Oh, how most of us remember our wedding, reception, and our honeymoon destination with fond memories (if we were fortunate enough to have a honeymoon). The newness of it all filled us with so much hope, joy, laughter, and intimacy (if we weren't burned out from having it before the wedding). If the intimacy was new to both husband and wife, then it was like being in heaven. When intimacy follows God's design, first entered into during marriage—ooh, la, la!

Yes, that act which we call sex is God's plan for us to become one with one another and one with Him. It is the act of our innermost spirit joining with one another. But so many humans have cheapened sex, entering into it so nonchalantly that it degrades the intimacy and the spiritual union it was intended to be.

Genesis 1:26-28 (KJV)
Then God said, "Let us make man in our image, after our likeness. And let them have dominion over the fish of the sea and over the birds of the heavens and over the livestock and over all the earth and over every creeping thing that creeps on the earth."

*So God created man in his own image,
in the image of God he created him;
male and female he created them.*

And God blessed them. And God said to them, "Be fruitful and multiply and fill the earth and subdue it and have dominion over the fish of the sea and over the birds of the heavens and over every living thing that moves on the earth."

As the Apostle Paul tells us:

1 Corinthians 7:28 (NIV © 2010)
But if you do marry, you have not sinned; and if a virgin marries, she has not sinned. But those who marry will face many troubles in this life, and I want to spare you this.

Marriage is a *SANCTIFIED UNION*, set aside for a specific purpose. This is why we should not be so quick to "fall in love," and make a commitment we cannot keep.

Proverbs 12:4 (KJV)
An excellent wife is the crown of her husband,
but she who brings shame is like rottenness in his bones.

Proverbs 18:22 (KJV)
He who finds a wife finds a good thing
and obtains favor from the Lord.

1 Peter 2:25-3:2 (KJV)
For you were straying like sheep, but have now returned to the
Shepherd and Overseer of your souls.

Likewise, wives, be subject to your own husbands, so that even if
some do not obey the word, they may be won without a word
by the conduct of their wives, when they see your respectful
and pure conduct.

Yes, we make mistakes on this journey of life, but if we are wise, we learn from our mistakes, and do not make them over and over again. If we continue to make the same mistakes over and over again, our life continues in a vicious cycle, coming right back to the state from which we began, never growing, never learning.

WHAT'S LOVE GOT TO DO WITH IT?

I am aware of the many reasons why people take the "leap" into marriage, but I question why—the evidence is in as to why not.

I'm not out to cheapen the feelings two people have toward one another, but simply must make the point that we must check ourselves to be sure the feelings we have that are leading us to marriage are not conditional. It takes two to make a marriage decision but it must always start with *ONE*, and that's *YOU*. We are only responsible for the part we, as an individual, play in the decisions we make.

After the honeymoon, then comes the marriage…

Yes, two people who plan to marry must have some kind of attraction to one another, that's a given, but in the end attraction isn't enough to get them through the hard times—and there will be hard times. *TRUE LOVE* isn't something you fall into; it grows like a flower. There is life in *TRUE LOVE*. It never fails.

Marriage is not a feeling, it is a commitment. That's why we must be very, very careful when we make a vow of marriage. We must be very careful when deciding to whom we say, "I do."

What I am speaking of is the casual way so many people enter into marriage relationships—then quit before the "bull is out of the yard," after making the vow. My comments are preventive measures, and after it's all said and done, "What's love got to do with it?"

The commitment you made to your spouse and to God supersedes how you might feel, or what you might think. We speak of a "happy" or "unhappy" marriage—that's conditional. We speak of finding happiness, and it is just as it says "happenstance" (what some call "*happenstance*")—it's circumstantial; can come and go. Life is truly what we make it, and it must first begin with us as individuals. Remember, you can have *PEACE* in the midst of a storm. It's what's on the inside of you that counts.

Since God's love is unconditional and we're entering into a union sanctioned by Him, why wouldn't we enter into it HIS way (or not at all)? And why wouldn't we depend on Him to turn things around? We must always remember He is a personal God who cares for us and our well-being. The changes that take place in us can changes our surroundings, situations or circumstances.

There will be instances when abuses, both physical and mental, take place in a marriage. Far be it from me to say that God would want anyone to put themselves in any harm or danger. God forbid. Even in a marriage situation where there is the *Down Low* (*DL*) scenario and a choice must be made, some stay and some leave. There will be times when one party wants the marriage and their spouse does not, but that has nothing to do with what marriage is or the sanctity of it.

The cause of divorce is usually the careless and carefree way the union is entered into. It is during the marriage when they make the hardest decisions. Without help from the Spirit of God which abides in us, our decisions will be selfish ones, regardless of which party is making the decision. Selfishness allows us to enter this union with plans to get out.

Why get married in the first place if you haven't COUNTED THE COST?

The kind of love we have a tendency to so flippantly speak of has much to do with our feelings (which is really lust), and not with what *LOVE IS*, for *LOVE is EVERLASTING*.

As the Apostle Paul tells us:

1 Corinthians 7:28 (NIV © 2010)
But if you do marry, you have not sinned; and if a virgin marries, she has not sinned. But those who marry will face many troubles in this life, and I want to spare you this.

Marriage is a *SANCTIFIED UNION*, set aside for a specific purpose. This is why we should not be so quick to "fall in love," and make a commitment we cannot keep.

As a friend of mine explained to me:

"What you say is true, however.....

How you feel about another person, is not necessarily flippantly "lust". Not in all cases. You can honestly LOVE another person, just like you love GOD, putting God first. Even in the beginning, when a man and woman first meet and seemingly fall in love, there is a certain amount of lust—even if it is not spoken or displayed between the two people for a long time. It cannot be avoided and is a natural attraction between a man and woman. Now when, and I stress WHEN you find that special man that you LOVE and he loves you—and you marry, it is up to the two of you to keep God's promise to love each other and be together forever. However, when we marry a mortal man or woman, we are not in essence marrying God, but God's promise. If only mortal man and woman could love God's way— wouldn't that be beautiful! Unfortunately, it takes two in a marital union to hold and keep God's promise. WHEN one strays or refuses to stay in a marriage... to me, it doesn't mean that either one or the other doesn't love God's way, it means that at this point, you need to make a choice to either stay in an unhappy marriage (where love has faded) by either one of the partners or leave. It doesn't mean that he or she did not really LOVE that person. It takes both partners loving GOD and respecting his rules of marriage as much as they love each other. If that is accomplished, yes—I think their love will be eternal to each other and God!

Just my opinion."

There is a place for our opinions, but when it comes to what "thus saith the Lord," our opinions have to take a back seat to God's instructions.

The foundation of marriage is based on the God kind of LOVE (AGAPE), love that is unconditional. This kind of love takes into account the fact that things will change, people will change, but after all is said and done—you will endure. You will persevere through it all.

You must realize that marriage is the union of two imperfect people, brought together for a sanctified purpose. A purpose that is totally different from those who are single.

God sees marriage as synonymous with His relationship with His church, the bride, the Body of Christ, and HE is the husbandman. He explicitly tells us how LOVE should behave.

1 Corinthians 13:4-8a (NIV © 2010)
Love is patient, love is kind. It does not envy, it does not boast,
it is not proud.

It does not dishonor others, it is not self-seeking, it is not easily
angered, it keeps no record of wrongs.

Love does not delight in evil but rejoices with the truth.

It always protects, always trusts, always hopes, always perseveres.

Love never fails.

In good times or bad times, God does not turn His back on us, and so must we—both husband and wife—not turn our backs on one another.

1 Peter 3:7 (KJV)
Likewise, husbands, live with your wives in an understanding way,
showing honor to the woman as the weaker vessel,
since they are heirs with you of the grace of life,
so that your prayers may not be hindered.

We must learn to weigh circumstances and situations in our marriage against the Word of God, so that we can make the correct decisions in marriage matters. For example, God would not ask us to remain in an abusive relationship. His Word tells us that He has prepared a way of escape for us out of any situation or circumstance that is not right or proper for us to be in—spiritual or natural. That's why it is imperative to know the Word of God so that we can think correctly when our back is up against the wall.

I believe a lot of our problems are because of our opinions and setting our selfish desires as a priority over truth. It's like that old cliché, "putting the cart before the horse." We are all too quick to jump the gun, failing to fully consider the consequences, possibilities, or probabilities involved in our decisions.

DIVORCE

Divorce is rampant and is occurring more now than it ever has. People are divorcing at the drop of a hat, without any thought, prayer, or reasoning. Most often, divorce is a selfish act. Those who desire it do so for selfish reasons. The decision to divorce should be followed with an introspection asking ourselves why we got married in the first place. And if we were married in church, before God and man, we should carefully consider again the vows we took at the time of our wedding ceremony.

Marriage is an institution, and just like "air" is just there and we enter into it. We don't create the rules, the rules are there and we agree to follow them. Many of us just cannot follow the rules. I guess some of us live by that old cliché, *"rules are meant to be broken,"* but that doesn't work in marriage, certainly not marriage the way God intended. Marriage is a *Principle* and principles are the foundation of life. We are to be a people of principle, a people of godly principle.

1 Corinthians 7:12-16 (NIV © 2010)
To the rest I say this (I, not the Lord): If any brother has a wife who is not a believer and she is willing to live with him, he must not divorce her.

*And if a woman has a husband who is not a believer
and he is willing to live with her, she must not divorce him.*

*For the unbelieving husband has been sanctified through his wife,
and the unbelieving wife has been sanctified through her
believing husband.
Otherwise your children would be unclean, but as it is, they are holy.*

*But if the unbeliever leaves, let him do so. A believing man or woman
is not bound in such circumstances;
God has called us to live in peace.*

*How do you know, wife, whether you will save your husband?
Or, how do you know, husband, whether you will save your wife?*

In Old Testament Scripture, adultery was addressed by Moses because God's people of that time had grown hard-hearted. Men were writing writs of divorce because it made it easier for them to commit adultery and have a clean conscious before God (or so they thought). So it is today in the hearts and minds of people. We want divorce so that we can do what we want to do.

Marriage is not about you, it is about the other person. If both of you consider the wants and needs of the other party above your own, you will find that your wants and needs are taken care of. Yes, it's just that simple. God never said it would be easy, but he sure made it simple.

In marriage, change is definitely going to come—to you and your spouse. If we were to handle our marriage trials and tribulations as God would have us to, we will not only please God, but it will be the best possible thing we can do for our mate, ourselves, and our marriage. Your relationship with God in a marriage is not about your spouse; it's about you. You will learn that no matter the situation or circumstance, if you decide to handle it the way God would have you to, things around you will change for the betterment of everyone involved.

1 John 4:18-20 (KJV)
There is no fear in love; but perfect love casteth out fear:
because fear hath torment.
He that feareth is not made perfect in love.

We love him, because he first loved us.

If a man say, I love God, and hateth his brother, he is a liar:
for he that loveth not his brother whom he hath seen, how can
he love God whom he hath not seen?

Apostle Paul tells us:

1 Corinthians 7:32-34 (NIV © 2010)
But I would have you without carefulness. He that is unmarried
careth for the things that belong to the Lord,
how he may please the Lord:

But he that is married careth for the things that are of the world,
how he may please his wife.

There is difference also between a wife and a virgin.
The unmarried woman careth for the things of the Lord,
that she may be holy both in body and in spirit:
but she that is married careth for the things of the world,
how she may please her husband.

We take that walk into marital bliss without fully considering the ups and downs that lay before us. We fail to comprehend that marriage is a commitment between two imperfect people who will change over time—people who are perpetually getting to know one another.

Philippians 2:1-3 (KJV)
If there be therefore any consolation in Christ, if any comfort of love, if any fellowship of the Spirit, if any bowels and mercies,

Fulfil ye my joy, that ye be likeminded, having the same love, being of one accord, of one mind.

Let nothing be done through strife or vainglory; but in lowliness of mind let each esteem other better than themselves.

INTROSPECTION

The decision to marry is vitally important and intended to be a lifelong vow of commitment to another imperfect person. Before we enter into it, we must do some serious soul- searching, that is, a very close examination of ourselves, both spiritually and naturally. The consequence of the decision to marry will remain with you forever.

I remember when I excitedly told a former employer that I was getting married—my second one. He said, "I thought you only got married once." That has always stuck with me. At the time I wondered why he said it and what exactly he meant. Where did he come up with such nonsense? At least that is what I thought when I heard it. It pays to take into consideration the words of wisdom spoken by elders and those who have grown in truth with evidence to prove it.

After thorough introspection, it is best that your decisions and questions be brought to the table. You and your potential spouse should be able to sit and discuss the issues of married people, looking for agreement in *TRUTH*.

Ephesians 5:22-33 (KJV)
Wives, submit yourselves unto your own husbands,
as unto the Lord.

For the husband is the head of the wife, even as Christ is the head of the church: and he is the saviour of the body.

Therefore as the church is subject unto Christ, so let the wives be to their own husbands in every thing.

Husbands, love your wives, even as Christ also loved the church, and gave himself for it;

That he might sanctify and cleanse it with the washing of water by the word,

That he might present it to himself a glorious church, not having spot, or wrinkle, or any such thing; but that it should be holy and without blemish.

So ought men to love their wives as their own bodies. He that loveth his wife loveth himself.

For no man ever yet hated his own flesh; but nourisheth and cherisheth it, even as the Lord the church:

For we are members of his body, of his flesh, and of his bones.

For this cause shall a man leave his father and mother, and shall be joined unto his wife, and they two shall be one flesh.

This is a great mystery: but I speak concerning Christ and the church.

Nevertheless let every one of you in particular so love his wife even as himself; and the wife see that she reverence her husband.

Don't be afraid of marriage. It's an opportunity to share your life with someone. It's an act of unselfishness and commitment. It's not for the faint of heart but it may be for you.

THE GLORIOUS STATE: SINGLENESS

One might question why the state of singleness is "glorious" and why anyone would want to be alone. It is not a question of being alone, but becoming complete in one's self. Some can attest to the fact that being with someone is sometimes (let's say, a lot of times), like being by yourself. That's the irony of this whole notion of needing someone to complete you, or needing someone to make you feel worthy of life and the pursuit of happiness.

Let's look at what the Apostle Paul had to say on the matter.

1 Corinthians 7:35-40 (NIV © 2010)
I am saying this for your own good, not to restrict you,
but that you may live in a right way in undivided devotion to the Lord.

If anyone thinks he is acting improperly toward the virgin
he is engaged to, and if she is getting along in years and
he feels he ought to marry, he should do as he wants.
He is not sinning. They should get married.

But the man who has settled the matter in his own mind,
who is under no compulsion but has control over his own will,

*and who has made up his mind not to marry the virgin—
this man also does the right thing.*

*So then, he who marries the virgin does right, but he who does
not marry her does even better.*

*A woman is bound to her husband as long as he lives.
But if her husband dies, she is free to marry anyone she wishes,
but he must belong to the Lord.*

*In my judgment, she is happier if she stays as she is—
and I think that I too have the Spirit of God.*

Singleness is the state many of us tend to rush through—in a hurry to grow up too fast. Yes, we are single through childhood (that intended selfish state—no one to care about but ourselves); through adolescence (more concerned about what people think about us); and adulthood (more concerned about teaming up with someone else to make us feel good). Therein lies the downfall.

If we would learn to appreciate who we are and WHOSE we are; if we would learn to love ourselves before we look for someone else to love us; if we would get to know the creator of our souls in a way that would give us a solid foundation on which to begin our journey in life; life would be for us as it was intended.

We have a tendency to look everywhere outside of ourselves for love and acceptance. We fail to make connection with God, through Jesus the Christ (by inviting His Spirit to come in to rest, rule, and abide in us). Because of this, we do not receive clear instruction, direction, and guidance.

We are created to make a connection to the **SOURCE OF LIFE** and to be able to usher others along in the same way.

We are the Creator's helpers, witnesses, workmen, angels, guides—created to lead the way. If you are searching—you are a leader. This connection should be made before marriage, so that you are able to endure the issues of life that are inherent in most marriages.

There is no rush to get married, but time is of essence in deciding whose report will you believe — the God of Abraham, Isaac and Jacob, or the gods you now serve.

Step up to the front of the line. Today is your day... *FOR A TRANSFORMATION.*

I SURRENDER ALL

I have by no means exhausted all that the Word of God has to say about living an abundant life. It is up to you to study, examine, dissect, and grow in the things of the Lord.

If you are at a point in your life where you are not sure which end is up, or perhaps you are at the end of your rope, it's time to look to the hills from which comes your help. Your help comes from the Lord—yours and everyone else's. Now do not be deceived, there are many gods, so make sure you call on Jehovah, Father, through Jesus, the Christ. This book is intended as a catalyst to move you to acknowledge where your faith lies; and if it is misplaced, to cause you to ask, seek and knock so that you too would enter into the truth of God's Word, and to the truth of life.

1 John 4:1-8 (KJV)
Beloved, believe not every spirit, but try the spirits whether they are of God: because many false prophets are gone out into the world.

Hereby know ye the Spirit of God: Every spirit that confesseth that Jesus Christ is come in the flesh is of God:

And every spirit that confesseth not that Jesus Christ is come in the flesh is not of God: and this is that spirit of antichrist, whereof ye have heard that it should come; and even now already is it in the world.

Ye are of God, little children, and have overcome them: because greater is he that is in you, than he that is in the world.

They are of the world: therefore speak they of the world, and the world heareth them.

We are of God: he that knoweth God heareth us; he that is not of God heareth not us. Hereby know we the spirit of truth, and the spirit of error.

Beloved, let us love one another: for love is of God; and every one that loveth is born of God, and knoweth God.

He that loveth not knoweth not God; for God is love.

It's time for you to ask the Spirit of the Living God to come into your life, that is, to surrender your choices and your ways to the power that resides in that Spirit. You are actually allowing God's Spirit, which is the *Holy Spirit* (or *Holy Ghost*), to intercede in your life. Believe me; you will know it when you have taken this first and all-important step into becoming one with God. This new journey will be guided by the *Holy Spirit*. He will be a compass on the sea of life to light the way.

Psalm 119:104-105 (KJV)
Through thy precepts I get understanding: therefore I hate every false way.
Thy word is a lamp unto my feet, and a light unto my path.

God's Spirit is a lamp for revealing what you are dealing with in your present, and a light for what is in your future. God's Spirit will be your teacher and your guide. It is by His Spirit that you will be able to endure the trials and tribulations that lie before you. It is by His Spirit that you will have peace in the midst of turmoil—when everything around you is falling apart, you still can say, "It is well with my soul." It is by His Spirit that you will be able to love one another. It is by His Spirit that you will be able to discern and dispel darkness, in order to walk in the light of the Lord.

1 John 4:12-15, 20-21 (KJV)
No man hath seen God at any time. If we love one another,
God dwelleth in us, and his love is perfected in us.

Hereby know we that we dwell in him, and he in us,
because he hath given us of his Spirit.

And we have seen and do testify that the Father sent the Son
to be the Saviour of the world.

Whosoever shall confess that Jesus is the Son of God,
God dwelleth in him, and he in God.

If a man say, I love God, and hateth his brother, he is a liar:
for he that loveth not his brother whom he hath seen,
how can he love God whom he hath not seen?

And this commandment have we from him,
That he who loveth God love his brother also.

Tomorrow is not promised and the time is nigh to make the right choice in life. Choose you this day who you will serve! Whether it be the gods of Oprah and Dr. Phil, or the King of kings and the Lord of lords! Make your election sure!

A NEW BEGINNING—A NEW LIFE IN CHRIST

(That depends on you…)

MY PRAYER FOR YOU

It is with great humility and sincerity that I send this prayer out for those who have chosen to read this book. I pray that just as I found what I needed to come into myself, and acknowledge the fact that I was not alone, that you too will diligently seek, and you will find what we all need. When you find it, in the process you will find who you are. The pronoun "it" does not actually tell you what you are looking for, but it does indicate that you need to find something, and that something is your spiritual connection to a true and living God.

I pray that if you do not know God, through Jesus the Christ that you get to know Him who offers to pardon you from your sins.

I pray that you understand the gift of eternal life which is found only in Jesus.

I pray that you receive the baptism of the *Holy Spirit*.

I pray that you will allow the Spirit of God to rise up in you and communicate with your spirit so that you may be led by His Spirit and walk in His Spirit.

I pray that you receive the abundant life that is offered from God through Jesus.

I pray that you be saved today; then converted, then perfected to mature in the things of God.

I pray that you accept the Lord today while He can be found, for tomorrow is not promised.

This is my prayer; in Jesus Name. AMEN

ENDNOTES

[1]The Gospel According to Oprah, Marcia Z. Nelson, 2005.
[2]Samuel Butler, English novelist, essayist and critic, 1835-1902). BrainyQuote.com, Xplore Inc, 2011. http://brainyquote.com/quotes/quotes/s/samuelbutl122806.html, accessed February 15, 2011.

CPSIA information can be obtained at www.ICGtesting.com
Printed in the USA
242891LV00001B/45/P